Toronto Home Buyer's Financing Guide

Step-By-Step – From Application To Closing

Understanding Your Home Financing Options and Mortgage Features

Thomas Cook

MANY THANKS GO TO...

I've known and worked with George Christopoulos for almost 20 years and have always found him to be a superb professional in his field of mortgage financing.

Big thanks go to George for his input and review in the creation of this important book. You can reach him via the info below.

George Christopoulos
Principal Broker at Dominion Lending Centres Mortgage Watch

Mobile | **416-721-9299**
Office | 416-721-9299, Extension 223
Email | **George@YourMortgageWatch.ca**

Web | www.GeorgeChristopoulos.ca

Office Address

478 Cosburn Avenue
Toronto M4J 2N5

AS A TORONTO CONDO
OR HOUSE BUYER AND SELLER...

You might benefit greatly from reading one or both of these highly informative books too

Get a clear understanding about everything you need to know when buying a Toronto condo or house

Free download at...

UltimateHomeBuyersGuide.com

Thinking Of Selling Your Toronto Condominium?

This 'Insider Tips...' book is the complete guide to selling your condo for the most money possible!

Free download at...

GettingTheBestPrice.ca

ABOUT THE AUTHOR

Let's start off by giving you a little background about where I'm coming from in terms of experience and knowledge. I've been in the real estate industry since 1980. While originally with Royal LePage, I switched to RE/MAX Hallmark in 1983, where I have been working ever since.

Along with helping literally thousands of people to buy and sell their homes, over the years I've been involved in a number of other real estate related activities as well. For example, through the '80s I had a property management company and at times managed up to 350 single-family homes, duplexes, triplexes, condos, and small four- and eight-unit buildings, mainly for investors but often for people who were out of the city on a job transfer and wanted to maintain their existing residence.

That has provided some great insight into such things as tenant related issues, understanding of the Tenant Protection Act, and knowledge on how to design a really good rental application and a comprehensive lease. I find those things help today with clients who are interested in buying something that has a rental component to it — maybe the traditional basement rental apartment where the owner lives upstairs, or more likely today a downtown Toronto condominium suite.

I've renovated about twenty-five homes in Toronto, as well as building a triplex from the ground up in Riverdale. In 2008, I built a cottage in the Kawarthas that started with an uncleared lot. These experiences certainly provided some great insights into working with contractors, dealing with City Hall for building permits, and even on occasion going to the Committee of Adjustment or the OMB (Ontario Municipal Board) when obtaining a permit requires applying for a variance.

I find these experiences help with clients who might be interested in buying something that needs renovation or fix up work.

I can certainly offer advice and answer those kinds of questions for my clients — and many more.

For several years, I also had a mortgage company, which provided a lot of insight into mortgage financing and learning how to package the buyer's mortgage application to get clients the best possible rate and terms.

During my 37+ year career, my Team and I have helped over 2500 buyers and sellers reach their real estate goals. This achievement has earned me one of the highest RE/MAX sales production awards… the Circle Of Legends.

TORONTO'S REAL ESTATE TEAM MISSION STATEMENT

Our goal is to give you such an exceptional home selling or buying experience that you will feel compelled to tell all your friends and family about us.

We use our time each and every day to its fullest potential, always remembering that our clients pay us to work diligently to get their home sold, or find their next home for purchase.

We strive to deliver more value to you than you expect to receive and to provide uncompromising service based on integrity, fairness, knowledge, professionalism and enthusiasm.

Once your real estate transaction has been completed, we'd be honoured if you were to refer our services to everyone you know so they could share the same excellent experience you enjoyed.

Here's How To Get In Touch...

Thomas Cook
Real Estate Sales Representative @ RE/MAX Hallmark Realty Ltd
Brokerage

Mobile | 647-962-1650
Office | 416-465-7850

Web | LivingInToronto.com
Email | Thomas@LivingInToronto.com

Author of '**Inside Tips To Getting The Best Price**' designed specifically
for Toronto condominium owners and sellers and several other books and
reports.

Author | Ultimate Toronto Home Buyer's Guide
Author | Toronto Home Buyer's Financing Guide
Author | Free Government Money Report
Author | Guide To Downtown Toronto Condo Prices

Experience || Thousands of homes sold since 1980
Professional Designations || ABR, SRES
Awards || RE/MAX's 2ND highest award - Circle Of Legends
Charity Support || Over $117,500 contributed to the Toronto Sick Kids
Hospital
Speaker & Agent Coach || Delivering seminars and presentations to the
public and Realtors about buying and selling real estate since 1995.

IT'S A NEW MORTGAGE WORLD OUT THERE FOR CANADIANS

In the fall of 2016 The Bank of Canada imposed new regulations governing the banking system and changing the way Canadians qualify for mortgages.

Prior to November 30th 2016, Canadian home buyers fell into two basic categories... High Ratio buyers (with less than 20% down payment) or Conventional buyers (with greater than 20% down payment). The mortgage rates for these mortgages were essentially the same.

After the Bank of Canada changes on Nov 30th , Canadian home buyers are now categorized in four ways as "High Ratio", "Insured - Conventional" , "Uninsured – Conventional" and "Rentals or Refinances".

Each one of these categories has its own unique interest rate.

The lower rates are found in the "High Ratio" and "Insured - Conventional" categories with the High Ratio having the lowest rate.

As of **January 1, 2018**, the rules changed again. Now, any mortgage, regardless if the borrower has less than 20% or more than 20% down (or equity), must be first qualified at the Bank of Canada Rate.

This means that every home buyer must qualify at the Bank of Canada Rate (BoC) , currently 5.14% (or 2.0% above the offered 5-year rate, whichever is greatest), regardless of the actual rate being charged by the lender, and have a maximum amortization of 25 years.

Needless to say, qualifying for a mortgage has become increasingly complex.

Now more than ever home buyers should be using the services of a Mortgage Professional instead of someone in a bank branch who has a multitude of titles and job functions and does not focus exclusively on helping clients with their mortgage needs.

Mortgage brokers on the other hand have access to arrange their client's financing with not with just one institution but with many Canadian banks, Trust companies and insurance companies. They work for the client and not for the bank.

Mortgage loans which do not require that BoC qualifying rate are still available from several Trust companies and secondary lenders.

A good borrowing strategy might be… Be loyal to yourself and NOT to your bank.

So, read on, build your knowledge and, if you feel like I've added some value to you, please feel free to contact me anytime with your questions.

Thomas Cook
Real Estate Sales Representative

SO, YOU WANT TO BUY A HOME… NOW WHAT?

So you've made the decision to become a Toronto condo or house owner – that's terrific! But what's your next move?

Let's be honest, buying a Toronto house or condo is a major financial decision and it shouldn't be taken lightly.

Don't worry, you're just like many other first-time buyers. Most have no idea what they should do first after they make the decision to buy a home.

So what do you do initially? Start checking out neighbourhood homes online? Do you contact an agent, think about arranging mortgage financing or maybe just call mom and dad or a home owner friend and ask for advice?

Those all sound like good options that can get the ball rolling for you, but they might not be the best or smart place to start. Sorry mom and dad!

For most people, the home buying process just doesn't happen overnight. There are a lot of things to consider such as where your down payment is coming from, how large a mortgage do you qualify for, how large a total monthly payment do you feel comfortable with and finally, fitting all that information together with the help of a Realtor, deciding on what neighbourhoods are affordable for you.

CONTENTS

Buyer & Market Education		Putting Your Plan Together		Consultants & Advisors For Life	
Custom HOMEWatch Search	Review your HOMEWatch Listings and/or	Market Experience Tours and	Meet for a Buyer Consultation	Start looking at homes	Congratulations you're now a proud house or condo owner
Set up Market Experience Tours	Meet for a Starbucks Strategy Session	Get a full mortgage pre-approval	Define your Wish List and refine your home search criteria	Negotiate the offer Offer is accepted	
6-18 MONTHS	6-9 MONTHS	3-6 MONTHS	2-3 MONTHS	BUY TODAY!	+30-120 DAYS

CHAPTER 1
GET SOME TIMELINE GUIDANCE

Actually, it's never too early to start thinking about how much of a mortgage you might qualify for. Many people start looking at condos or houses online or at open houses 6-18 months ahead of when they're thinking they might actually buy.

Having a realistic figure in mind about how large of a mortgage you could get approved for will save you a lot of time (and dreaming).

Another good reason to get an early pre-approval is that, in all probability, you will find out things about your credit or about what you need income-wise that you didn't know before.

You can then use your lead time profitably to clear up any issues or solidify jobs or create a bigger down payment.

Certainly, before you start seriously looking for a home you'll want to talk to a mortgage professional and get a FULL mortgage pre-approval. We'll talk more about what that entails further on in this Guide.

CHAPTER 2
3 THINGS YOU ABSOLUTELY NEED TO BE A SUCCESSFUL BUYER

Cash, Cash, Cash...

You'll definitely need the big bucks to buy a house or condo in Toronto. For purchases up to $500,000, you'll need a minimum of 5% down payment and for purchases between $500K and $1,000,000 you'll need a minimum of 7% down, plus closing costs.

When asked by a bank lender or mortgage broker how much cash you have, give them an exact figure for your total and tell them that includes money you'll need for closing costs so there's no confusion.

Your down payment can come from your bank account, your RRSP, any GICs or Term Deposits or from the bank of Mom and Dad or any combination thereof.

Income... Real Money From An Employer Or Business

It may seem obvious but mortgage approvals are calculated based on your income, not on the property in the vast majority of situations.

The only way to show your ability to repay a mortgage is to prove that you have enough money coming in via employment letters, pay stubs and your tax returns.

Generally speaking, you'll need to verify that you have enough income to offset the mortgage payment and to keep your debts relatively low in relationship to your income, which creates room for your mortgage payment.

Self-employed people often keep their stated income for tax purposes very low to avoid paying tax but this ends up biting them in the butt when they go to apply for a mortgage and can't prove that they have the income to qualify for a higher loan.

First Thing's First – Make Sure You Have Good Credit

Many home buyers don't understand how important having good credit is when considering purchasing a condo or house.

The home-buying process begins well before you start physically looking for real estate. A credit score, which significantly impacts the home financing process, is built on good spending habits and a pattern of responsible borrowing established over a lifetime.

One of the biggest factors banks and mortgage brokers consider when qualifying you for a mortgage is your credit score. We understand, trying to figure out your credit score can be confusing and even a bit overwhelming, but the reality is that you can easily monitor your credit profile.

Check Your Beacon Credit Score

Credit scores are not used to predict how rich or poor you are. The point of credit scores is to measure how likely you are to be able to repay a loan. Everyone who's ever borrowed money to buy a car or a house or applied for a credit card or any other personal loan has a credit file.

Because we love to borrow money, that means almost every adult Canadian has a credit file. More than 21 million Canadians have credit reports. And most of us have no idea what's in them.

Are there mistakes? Have you been denied credit and don't know why? Is someone trying to steal your identity? A simple check of your credit report will probably answer all those questions.

You may be surprised by the amount of personal financial data in your credit report. It contains information about every loan you've taken out in the last six years — whether you regularly pay on time, how much you owe, what your credit limit is on each account and a list of authorized credit grantors who have accessed your file.

Credit score numbers can range from 300 to 900. The higher the number, the better. For example, a number between 750 to 799 is shared by 27 per cent of the population.

In addition to an overall score, your credit bureau account includes a notation that includes a letter and a number relating to all your debt history. The letter "R" refers to a revolving debt, while the letter "I" stands for an instalment account.

The numbers go from 0 (too new to rate) to 9 (bad debt or placed for collection or bankruptcy.) For a revolving account, an R1 rating is the notation to have. That means you pay your bills within 30 days, or "as agreed."

When banks and other lenders are trying to figure out whether or not to approve you for a loan, they rely heavily on credit scores. That makes healthy credit vital if you want access to financing.

There are all kinds of new and easy ways to monitor your credit score. The simplest in Toronto is through Equifax, one of the two predominant credit scorers we have. You can go to their site at www.Equifax.com and arrange to get your own score for minimal cost.

It's an easy way to view your credit profile and identify possible problem areas that are holding your credit score back.

Credit scores are a crucial component of the home-buying process, impacting everything from the size of a mortgage payment to the interest rate on a home loan.

People with subprime credit may face financial barriers to homeownership, making it difficult for their dream home to become a reality.

If you have a credit score below 640, it's advantageous to take the time to improve your credit score before looking to secure your home loan. Not only will that likely save you thousands in monthly interest, but taking that time will offer a clearer picture of how you can save for a down payment as well.

If you apply for a mortgage loan with a spouse or partner, the lender will look at both scores. It's important to work together to improve both of your scores before you take on a joint mortgage application.

All of these components must be in alignment in order to qualify for mortgage financing.

CHAPTER 3
4 SIGNIFICANT SIGNS YOU'RE NOT READY FOR A MORTGAGE

Toronto's real estate market has been going steadily upward since 1997 and, although 2017 had exceptional appreciation above 20%, the average has been about 7% over the last several years.

Bullish outlook aside, there are still plenty of challenges for many would-be buyers, from shaky credit to sputtering incomes and more. To be sure, the right time to pursue a home purchase is when you're financially and emotionally ready.

Here's a look at a few signs you may not quite be there.

Bruised Or Beaten Credit

Consumers with scores below 620 can have a tougher time securing mortgage financing. You might need to work on improving that first.

Insufficient Savings

Since Toronto and the GTA have seen steady price increases, the minimum down payment needed has grown also. Besides a 5-7% down payment requirement, you'll have to pay additional cash to cover closing costs. Count on closing costs to average another 2% of the purchase price.

There are excellent, unconventional ways to add quickly to your down payment described later in this Home Buyer's Financing Guide.

Income Instability

Mortgage lenders want to feel like you're a safe bet. A rocky employment situation can raise red flags.

Ideally, you've been working the same job for at least the last two years. But that's certainly not a reality for many Canadian workers.

Employment scenarios are always a case-by-case evaluation.

Generally, though, you might have a tougher time securing a mortgage if:

- You've been on the job less than a year
- You've been self-employed for less than two years
- You're a commission-based employee without a two-year track record
- You've recently changed career fields or had a lengthy job gap.

CHAPTER 4
HOW TO AVOID A BAD CREDIT RATING

It may not be great now, but with a little effort—and admittedly, a lot of time—you can give your credit score a big boost.

Once a collection item hits your credit score, the damage is done. With your FICO score, the only thing that can heal your score is time.

So how do you improve your credit score? Everybody's situation is different but here are few guidelines you need to take to heart.

- Pay your bills (credit cards, car loans etc) on time - at least make the minimum payment on time and pay more with your next pay check. We know… that's obvious but paying late by even 30 days could lower your score by between 20-40 points.

- Keep balances for credit cards and lines of credit under 35% of your revolving credit limit. The best way to earn a healthy credit score is by keeping your utilization low. Carrying a balance won't necessarily hurt your score, so long as you are using less than 35% of your total available credit limit across all your credit card accounts.

- Apply for and open new credit accounts only as needed. Don't open accounts just to have a better credit mix. It probably won't improve your credit score. When a lender or business checks your credit, it causes a hard inquiry to your credit file which often will 'cost' you credit score points. Apply for new credit in moderation.

- Pay off debt rather than move it around. Also, don't close unused cards as a short-term strategy to improve your credit score. Owing the same amount but having fewer open accounts may lower your credit score.

Set Realistic Goals

Putting down a larger down payment will lower your monthly mortgage payment, but don't put down more than you can afford.

You'll need to plan for more than just that down payment, too.

Keep in mind that you will need money for closing costs, land transfer tax, etc. before you can purchase your home – I'll cover closing costs in a later chapter.

CHAPTER 5
HOW TO GET AN AWESOME NEW CREDIT RATING

If you are thinking about buying a home and obtaining a mortgage, one of the first things to consider is your personal credit rating. Building a good credit history is important. If you have no reported credit history, it may take time to establish your first account.

This problem affects young people just beginning careers as well as older people who have never used credit. It also affects divorced or widowed spouses who shared credit accounts and were reported only in the other spouse's name.

You may also have poor credit or a recent bankruptcy and need to restore your credit profile. Do not apply for a loan, or even think of obtaining a mortgage until you have firmly established or re-established your credit.

The fastest way to establish or re-establish your credit is with a Secured Credit Card

Secured credit cards require a security deposit and typically the credit limit is set at the amount of your deposit. You can put down as little as $500 up to $5,000.

Your security deposit will earn interest while your card remains in good standing. If you cancel your card and pay off the balance, you will get back your security deposit and the interest accrued.

All credit cards, whether they are regular bank cards, department store cards, secured or unsecured credit cards are reported to your credit bureau and all activities are updated monthly.

A secured credit card will give you the opportunity to establish your credit on your personal credit report. Small private loans, or loans for used cars from your local used car dealer will not help re-establish your credit, because these types of loans are NOT reported to the credit bureaus.

Currently, most Canadian banks fall behind when it comes to providing help to establish or re-establish credit. Many individuals with poor credit history are declined when applying for major credit cards. Some banks offer a secured credit card, but they may require up to three times the amount of deposit for security. This means that if you need $500 credit limit you would have to deposit as much as $1,500.

Benefits Of The Right Secured Credit Card

As well as helping to establish a good credit rating, the benefits of a secured card are many:

Accepted at over 450,000 Canadian locations and over 16 million around the world

- Cash advances available at over 718,000 ATM's around the world displaying the VISA logo

- Your security deposit earns interest

- The amount of your security deposit is equal to your credit limit

- You can rent your favourite movies, car, hotel room, make purchases over the phone or the internet and most of all, **start establishing your credit**!

CHAPTER 6
WILL APPLYING FOR A MORTGAGE NEGATIVELY AFFECT YOUR CREDIT SCORE?

When you apply for a mortgage, you must have your credit checked. It is the only way a mortgage company can really determine whether you can qualify for financing and what your rates and fees will look like.

If you are applying for multiple forms of credit at the same time, such as a credit card, a mortgage and an auto loan, such actions will negatively impact your credit score.

Each of these applications will generate a hard inquiry on your credit report, which could send a signal to lenders that you are having difficulty managing credit.

But you can avoid extra damage to your credit score if you apply for one form of credit at a time, and limit the time between each credit inquiry.

That's because most credit scoring models group credit inquiries for the same type of financing (mortgage, credit cards or lines of credit) that are made within a specific timeframe to allow people to comparison-shop for competitive rates.

It can vary from model to model, but, in most cases, all inquiries of one of those types will be counted as one, provided they take place within a 14- to 45-day period.

A single inquiry is likely to drop your score by less than five points.
As an industry, mortgage brokers use a single secure system and can send that ONE credit report to multiple lenders if needed. That five-point effect on your credit will rebound within a month. This allows for one-stop shopping with minimal impact on your credit score.

CHAPTER 7
AVOID MAKING THESE 5 COMMON MORTGAGE APPLICATION MISTAKES

These **Absolute Do Nots** while applying for a mortgage AND up until closing are so important that any one of them can easily bring a mortgage approval or closing to a screeching halt.

The 5 Absolute DO NOTs while applying for a mortgage are:

- **DON'T** go out and buy a new car, furniture or ANY other large purchase. If you obtain any new debt (lease or bank loan) while your loan is in process AND until you get the keys to your new condo or house, you will be asked to document any new payments and those payments will be added into your mortgage qualification calculations. This new payment could put you over the edge and you may no longer qualify for the mortgage you want.

- **DON'T** stop making payments on your monthly bills such as credit cards, auto loan or lease payments, etc. Often mortgage lenders will rerun your credit just before closing and any recent late payments (or new debts) could not only drop your credit score, but, also make you ineligible for financing as some mortgage lenders have minimum credit score requirements.

- **DON'T** apply for any new credit cards or any other loans while you have a mortgage application in process. Not only could this lower your credit score, but also as mentioned above, obtaining any new debt could result in you no longer qualifying for the mortgage.

- **DON'T** make any large bank deposits or transfers that you can't document and explain. I repeat **DO NOT** make any large deposits or transfers you can't document. Any large deposit or transfer may require additional documentation and could delay your closing.

- **DON'T** quit your job, even if it's for a better one, during the home buying process. A change in jobs will almost always require you to be in a 90-day probationary period by that new employer. Mortgage lenders will not advance funds if you're still in that probationary time.

CHAPTER 8
HOW MUCH MORTGAGE CAN YOU AFFORD...
CRUNCH THE NUMBERS

How Far Will Your Money Go At Today's Rates?

Amortization schedules, 3.19 per cent five-year, closed rate, bi-weekly payments... you might know all these mortgage terms by now, but have you sat down and figured out how much condo or house your money will buy?

With the help of our mortgage calculator, it's easy to figure out! We're going to go through a little exercise using a five-year mortgage rate as an example. We're choosing that term because about 90 per cent of our first-time buyer 'Clients For Life' opt for it. They tend to enjoy the added security of knowing what their mortgage rate will be for five years.

We're also going to base the example on a 25-year amortization schedule, which means that it would take 25 years to pay off your mortgage. This is also the most common choice among our "first timers."

We'll have to pick a rate for example purposes, but you can check on current rates on the mortgage rates page at **YourMortgageWatch.ca**. Keep in mind that we have ties with mortgage professionals who routinely shave an entire percentage point or more from the bank's posted rate for our 'Clients For Life.' If you're a good negotiator, you may be able to negotiate this yourself with your branch manager.

We're going to choose a five-year rate of 3.19% for our example.

Well, now that we've established the rate and the amortization, let's look at different mortgage amounts and what they cost monthly. A $100,000 mortgage would cost you ... drum roll please... $483 a month in principal and interest payments (a fancy way of saying the WHOLE mortgage payment.)

Did you expect that figure to be much, much higher? Sometimes our buyers are shocked to learn just how far their money will go. Perhaps some of you have heard horror stories from leading-edge Baby Boomers who paid 16, 17 or 18 per cent for mortgages in the early '80s.

For argument's sake, a $100,000 mortgage at 17 per cent costs $1,437.80 a month. That number is even more shocking when you compare it to the monthly cost for a $400,000 mortgage at today's available rate—$1,932.

To add yet another bit of perspective to these figures, for many of our first-time buyers, that mortgage payment of $1,932 monthly is not much more than the rent that they already pay -- and sometimes it's less. Is it less than what you pay?

We don't want to mislead you, though. You must still add expenses such as realty taxes, utilities, condo maintenance fees, insurance and the like to your monthly mortgage payment when you buy your own home, but you're also building equity. And you don't have to face yearly rent increases!

If what you've just read intrigues you and you'd like to know more about what you can and can't afford, you can ask us about our free mortgage analysis—connect with us online or by phone and we will get back to you about which mortgage suits your needs best.

Get your free Mortgage Consultation analysis by calling George Christopoulos at 416-721-9299 Extension 221 OR online at **GeorgeChristopoulos.ca/how-to-apply-mortgage**.

You can call us any time directly with your mortgage questions, or you can drop him an email to **George@YourMortgageWatch.ca**.

MORTGAGE QUALIFICATION CHART – LEARN HOW MUCH YOU CAN BORROW

As of **January 1 2018** all new mortgages (regardless of down payment amount) in Canada MUST have a stress test applied to them at the time of approval.

Regardless of the actual interest rate being offered by a lender, the borrower MUST qualify for the new mortgage at the Bank Of Canada (BoC) Rate OR the rate offered the consumer PLUS 2%.

This 'Affordability Chart' is based on the borrower's gross income and using the current Bank Of Canada rate of 5.19%. If the 'actual' mortgage rate being offered to the borrower is higher than 3.19%, then the borrower will automatically have to qualify at that rate PLUS 2.0%.

For example, if the offered rate is 3.49%, then the 'qualifying rate' used would be 5.49% - and the size of mortgage the borrower could qualify for would be less than the numbers shown on the chart below.

Income	Mortgage Qualifying Amount (BoC = 5.19%)
$60,000	$255,000
$70,000	$305,000
$80,000	$354,000
$90,000	$400,000
$100,000	$447,000
$110,000	$493,000
$120,000	$548,000
$130,000	$603,000
$140,000	$657,000
$150,000	$794,000
$200,000	$953,000
$225,000	$1,075,000
$250,000	$1,160,000
$275,000	$1,270,000
$300,000	$1,400,000
$400,000	$1,900,000
$500,000	$2,200,000

CHAPTER 9
IF YOU HAVE LESS THAN 20% DOWN PAYMENT OR CAN QUALIFY USING THE NEW STRESS TEST FOR LOWER RATES...

New Bank of Canada rules that came out in October / November of 2016 and then in January 2018 changed a lot of details about how large of a mortgage both high-ratio borrowers with less than 20% down AND borrowers with more than 20% down can be approved for.

Take a look at the right-hand column of the chart above titled "BoC Chart @ 5.14%". The Bank of Canada (BoC) has dictated that high-ratio borrowers must qualify at the BoC rate determined by them, even if you can get a mortgage for 2% less.

As an example, look at the amount you qualify for if you earned $100,000 annually either by yourself or combined with a partner. If the interest rate was 3.19%, before the fall of 2016 you would have qualified for a mortgage of approximately $495,000 but under the new rules you would only qualify for $447,000.

This reduces your available mortgage by $48,000.

So why did the Bank of Canada do this? In their view, there is a distinct possibility that interest rates might rise in the coming years as they did during 2017.

We have been in a 'low rate' situation now for 8-10 years now and odds are that something domestically or globally will cause rates to rise.

It's probably a good thing that they're preparing for a worst-case scenario and endeavoring to prevent a future implosion in our Canadian real estate market if rates were to rise.

CHAPTER 10
EASY AND MOST EFFECTIVE AFFORDABILITY MEASUREMENT

Creating a budget before you buy a condo or house is crucial to keeping your financial house in order.

You don't want to get yourself into a situation where you are 'house poor' and not able to enjoy your new home.

You'll want to consider every expense that you currently incur monthly to see where you spend your money now and then work out where you might be able to save money and cash flow in the future.

Remember, it's only human nature to downplay how much things cost, but resist the impulse.

Be realistic about what you spend daily, weekly and monthly, because if the final figure is underestimated, you could find yourself in a financial bind once the home mortgage payments, realty taxes, utility and maintenance costs are all a reality.

It's important to structure your monthly expenses so that you can still afford some simple luxuries, occasional vacation time and still have money available for unexpected expenses when they occur.

See the **Appendix** for a hard copy of the budget calculation form and work out what your budget numbers are.

CHAPTER 11
AVOID ANXIETY WHEN APPLYING FOR A FULL MORTGAGE PRE-APPROVAL

A pre-approval VS a **full mortgage pre-approval**... they sound the same but they're very different.

Every Realtor has had a client who thinks they have been pre-approved only to find out they cannot qualify for the homes they have been looking at.
Often this does not become clear until the buyer has wasted way too much of their time looking at properties they have no chance of qualifying for.

And often clients get a pre-approval certificate from a bank that has a long list of conditions attached.

What many banks do when qualifying a buyer for a mortgage is to just ask a few basic questions such as, "What is your annual income?", and, "What are your debts?". The problem is that the banker or mortgage broker is relying on verbal information that may be inaccurate or that may not meet today's new mortgage guidelines.

Then they will give you one of two things... a verbal quotation on how much you can borrow OR a written "Quick Qualifier".

The problem with both of these is that they are conditional upon three things... you supplying satisfactory proof of income & down payment and you having a satisfactory credit bureau.

Basically you have nothing until all three of the bank's conditions have been met!

A FULL mortgage pre-approval goes much deeper... and many bank reps don't want to spend the time up front with the buyer unless they're guaranteed to get the mortgage business.

Getting a full mortgage pre-approval means you need to provide up front all of the documentation... proof of income, proof of down payment and get your credit bureau done... all ahead of time.

The client is asked not only how much their income is BUT how that income is earned. Full time/part time/over time/contract/self-employed. All of this information is reviewed and considered differently at the time of mortgage approval.

The source(s) of your down payment are reviewed and a credit bureau report is looked at.

When completed, the client's personal covenant has been reviewed and an accurate budget established based on what they want to spend and what the banks will lend them.

If a client needs a guarantor or a co-signer, they find out right away, not when they have made an offer and wasted countless hours of their time.

Of course, obtaining a great interest rate is an important part of this process too.

This is the highest rate you would pay. Your mortgage broker is only beginning to work for you since the lowest rates are often not offered until 45 days prior to your closing date and are not available with a pre-approval.

Remember... you'll need to supply all of this personal information anyway so it's to your advantage to provide it up front ahead of time.

Once you have full mortgage pre-approval in place it is just like having a credit card with a set limit to go and buy a condo or house. Now you know yourself that if you have a credit card with a limit of $5,000, you can confidently go out and buy something for up to $5,000 without question.

It's the same thing here! By getting that full mortgage pre-approval in place, it's like having a credit card to go out have a mortgage of up to $500,000 or whatever your number is.

If you add on the down payment that you have, let say $40,000, then you can buy up to a purchase price of $540,000.

It's a tremendous value just having that mortgage 'credit card' in place so that you know for sure exactly how much you can purchase!

There are two major benefits to doing this ahead of time... First you now know without question exactly how large of a mortgage you can qualify for and secondly, there will be NO stress once you buy that your mortgage will not be approved. Just add on your down payment and you know the maximum price you can pay.

Many people mistakenly believe that by just filling in an online form or having a conversation with a banker where they verbally provide data about their income and their debts is enough to go out and buy a condo or house.

A quick qualifier is ABSOLUTELY not enough and it's very dangerous to buy any home based on just this.

To be 100% sure of your financial capability, and get a **FULL mortgage pre-approval**, a prospective buyer must provide their banker or mortgage broker with proof of income, proof of down payment and have a credit bureau done. Here's what you'll need to provide...

1.   **A completed mortgage application form**

2.   For **proof of income**, you'll provide a copy of your employment letter, a current pay stub and your last income tax return with T4s and Notice Of Assessment from Revenue Canada (CRA)

     If you are self-employed, you'll need to provide a copy of three years of CRA tax assessment statements.

3.   For **proof of down payment**, you'll provide a copy of any GICs, term deposits, or RRSPs plus a copy of your bank statement showing current cash in the bank. If you're getting funds from a family member, you'll need to provide a copy of a gift letter signed by that person.

Your lender or mortgage broker will then do a credit check and they will issue an Unconditional Pre-Approval Certificate, which is the lender's guaranteed mortgage commitment to the buyer.

It is conditional only upon an appraisal or CMHC/GE Capital high-ratio mortgage insurance approval.

CHAPTER 12
HOW MUCH DOES CMHC MORTGAGE LOAN INSURANCE COST?

Canada Mortgage And Housing Corporation (CMHC) is the publicly owned corporation which provides mortgage insurance to borrows, most of whom have high ratio mortgages above 80% loan-to-value (LTV).

This insurance does not benefit you directly… it protects the lenders in case a borrower defaults on their mortgage payments and the bank has to take the property back under Power Of Sale.

To obtain CMHC Mortgage Loan Insurance, lenders pay an insurance premium. Typically, your lender will pass these costs on to you. Your lender will give you the exact insurance cost when you apply for a mortgage.

The CMHC Mortgage Loan Insurance premium is calculated as a percentage of the loan and is based on the size of your down payment.

The higher the percentage of the total house price/value that you borrow, the higher percentage you will pay in insurance premiums.

Remember: without mortgage insurance you may avoid the insurance premium but you might have to pay a somewhat higher interest rate and additional administrative fees.

At the end of the day, for the vast majority of borrowers, the cost of CMHC Mortgage Loan Insurance is more than fully offset by the savings achieved.

CMHC Premiums Chart – Effective March 2018

Loan-To-Value	CMHC Premium On Total Loan
Up to & including 65%	0.60%
65% to 75%	1.70%
75% to 80%	2.40%
80% to 85%	2.80%
85% to 90%	3.10%
90% to 95%	4.00%

Down Payment Requirements — Traditional sources of down payment include: Applicant's savings, RRSP withdrawal, funds borrowed against proven assets, proceeds from the sale of another property or a non-repayable gift from immediate relative.

In almost all cases, the CMHC insurance premium is added onto the principal balance of your mortgage (no extra cash needed on closing to pay for this).

CMHC Premiums in Ontario are subject to provincial sales tax. The provincial sales tax amount cannot be added to the loan amount and must be paid as part of the buyer's closing costs.

CHAPTER 13
VARIABLE RATE VERSUS FIXED-RATE MORTGAGES

There are two major types of mortgages offered to buyers in Canada. The most common is the fixed-rate mortgage which has an interest rate that does not change over the term of the mortgage… typically one to five years.

A fixed-rate mortgage offers security to the buyer because the rate that they were approved for and can afford will not change during that time.

A variable-rate mortgage rate has the ability to float with the Prime rate and may go up or down depending on the state of our economy and the Canadian dollar. The rate is set at Prime plus or minus a small percentage. This rate at the initial point of starting your mortgage will usually be less than the fixed rate for the most common 5-year term.

However you have no control over whether it goes up or down from there. I've seen situations where our Prime rate went up a year after the mortgage was set and the borrowers ended up paying a higher interest rate than what they could have had as a fixed rate. I've also seen the reverse happen!

Every variable rate mortgage has a mechanism built into it to protect the borrower in the event the Prime Rate rises.

Should the Prime Rate rise, most variable rate mortgages will automatically increase the mortgage payment to ensure the amortization continues reducing and NOT increasing.

The reverse occurs should the Prime Rate drop as it did in 2015. The borrower's payment actually dropped. Your bank or lender is obligated to notify you of any change in Prime if that happens.

While the lower payment nice to have. Why not take advantage of it.

Every February, George asks his clients to send him their Annual Mortgage statements and he reviews them and looks for ways they could pay down their mortgage sooner.

This could be a simple reminder to make accelerated weekly or bi-weekly payments, increase their payments or to use their potential income tax refund to reduce their mortgage principal.

This year another savings method became quite clear after reviewing statements from clients who have a variable rate mortgage and their payment went down.

To take advantage of this savings method, contact your bank or lender and ask that the payment be returned to the original amount. This is available with most mortgages through one of the pre-payment options built into the mortgage. This amount can vary from 10%-20% of your original mortgage principal.

Have a look at your most recent Annual Mortgage Statement (usually mailed to you by your lender before the end of January) and compare the current payment to the original payment, or contact me to assist you in reviewing the statements.

Here is another little tip for you… increasing your payment by 10% annually and paying your mortgage on an accelerated bi-weekly basis will pay off a 25-year mortgage in 10-14 years.

Increasing 10% every year may be a tough but remember that any pre-payment you make (lump sum or monthly / bi-weekly) will lower that amortization for you and save you a lot ultimately on interest.

CHAPTER 14
BRIDGE FINANCING – A SOLUTION WHEN BUY
AND SELL DATES DON'T MATCH UP

If you want to sell your current home and use the proceeds as a down payment on a different property, what do you do if the closing dates don't fall on the same day? More to the point, what do you do if you have to close on your new home before you sell the old one?

In these situations, you'll need a short-term loan to bridge the gap between the two transaction dates and the solution, appropriately enough, is called bridge financing. Here's how it works for borrowers who are considering this option.

Let's start by addressing a few common concerns. If you need a bridge loan, it does not alter or limit your ability to qualify for a mortgage in any way. Also, you typically don't actually need to qualify for bridge financing itself – the only, and critical, requirement is that you have an unconditional offer to purchase for the property you are selling.

It is almost always offered in combination with a traditional mortgage loan – your lender simply bridges your financing gap to help facilitate the overall transaction. So you would not have your main mortgage financing on your new home with a different lender than the one supplying the bridge funds.

In Toronto's busy market, it is often prudent to purchase a new home first and then put your home on the market after you've found one. The reason? It's an exceptionally strong seller's market in many city neighbourhoods with multiple offers happening almost 60+% of the time.

Many times, our buyers have put in offers on homes they liked and were beaten out by a higher offer. The buying process sometimes stretches out to two to three months before you make a winning bid.

Imagine if you've already sold your home with a typical 60-day closing... if you'd sold first, you might find yourself homeless or feeling rushed to buy something you didn't really like.

In situations like this, we always advise our seller / buyer clients to talk up front with their mortgage lender about arranging bridge financing so they understand the process perfectly.

Another frequent reason to bridge is if the home you're buying needs some fix-ups before you move in... maybe painting, a new kitchen, hardwood floors installed etc. Since these are sometimes messy jobs and no fun to live through, many buyers prefer to get these jobs done before moving in.

So now let's assume you buy a new property for $650,000 with a $50,000 deposit with your offer, and the sellers want you to take possession on October 12, which is 60 days away. You now immediately get your home listed and on the market for sale.

A week later, we get an unconditional offer on your existing home. The price is excellent ($450,000), in fact it's higher than you anticipated, but the closing that the buyer wants is October 30th... 18 days after the purchase date of your new home.

Since the offer on your existing home is firm without conditions, your mortgage lender will love you and will work with you to set up the bridge loan.

On October 12th, your lender will advance a total of $600,000 (Purchase price of $650,000 less your $50,000 offer deposit) to buy your new home. The interest rate for the 18 days is typically Prime + 2-3% and, because it's for such a short time, doesn't typically amount to very much of an expense.

Then on October 30th, once you've closed on your old home, the net funds from that sale are applied to pay down the $600,000 bridge loan and you're left with your final first mortgage amount.

Lenders typically expect a gap of no more than 30 days between your buy and sell dates, although bridges for longer periods may be offered by some lenders on an exception basis.

Keep in mind that, on balance, bridge loan rates will have far less impact on your overall financing costs than mortgage rates because they only apply on the shortfall, and they are only in place for a brief period of time.

If you have borrowing room on any existing lines of credit, most lenders will ask you to draw down these lines first, before then bridging the remaining gap.

On the day you complete the purchase of your new home, you will be required to sign a Letter of Direction and Irrevocable Assignment of Funds directing your lawyer to use your net sale proceeds to pay off the lender's bridge loan before taking any money for yourself.

On larger bridge loans, your lender may go a step further and require that a collateral charge be registered on the property you are selling (this is a slightly more expensive step that achieves the same basic end).

While not all lenders offer bridge financing, an experienced, independent mortgage broker will have access to several who do.

So instead of worrying about lining up your closing dates on the same day and trying for perfection in an imperfect world, use bridge financing as an easy and cost-effective tool when coordinating buying and selling transactions.

CHAPTER 15
PROTECT YOUR FAMILY WITH MORTGAGE LIFE INSURANCE

Sometimes we're quite laissez-faire about making sure we're protected in case of the death of ourselves or a family member.

I've had a situation where a father and son bought a rental property together with the son living in one of the units. The father made sure he was insured but, because he thought his son would outlive him, he didn't insure his son's life.

You can see where this is going… about six months later the son was killed in an automobile accident and that left the father in a precarious position. He was now forced to take over all the payments on that property and he had to really stretch to do that.

If you've got a wife and family, you definitely need to make sure everyone is protected in the case of an accident or unforeseen illness occurring. The time to do this is either before you purchase a home together or at the time of purchase.

The best way to get this insurance is to contact a life insurance specialist. They'll go over all the options between term and life policies and you can pick the coverage and type that's best for you.

Since life often gets in the way and we sometimes don't pay enough attention to arranging for our loved ones to be protected, mortgage lenders offer an easy solution.

At the time when you sign your mortgage documents with your lender, they will offer you the option of adding life insurance to your mortgage payment. The bank's life insurance covers just the outstanding principal amount of the mortgage and, in the event of the death of any of the home owners, the mortgage would be paid off in full.

Talk to your mortgage broker or bank lender to check on coverage and costs. Even if you think that you'll get in touch with your insurance agent later, I'd suggest you sign up for the bank's insurance at the time of purchase. You may not get around to that conversation with the life insurance agent before it's too late!

CHAPTER 16
WORRIED ABOUT GETTING A MORTGAGE APPROVAL IF YOU'RE SELF-EMPLOYED?

Being self-employed (Business-For-Self or BFS in industry terms) can make it challenging to be approved for any type of financing.

You are considered to be a BFS applicant if you own the majority of a company, are on contract or are running a business where you are a sole practitioner.

Because the BFS applicant's declared (for tax purposes) income is sometimes a fraction of their real total income, it often becomes difficult to determine the client's true income.

Credit card companies and banks ask many more questions of a BFS applicant than if you are employed by a company on a fixed salary with a strong employment history. Mortgage lenders are no different BUT there are still plenty of options.

As with any mortgage, there are three main sources of funds... banks, Trust Companies, Credit Unions and private funds with the banks having the best rates and private funds being the most expensive.

Since a BFS client's 'real' income is often hard to determine, each lender has their own way of determining what income from their tax returns to consider when considering an approval.

Banks require that the applicant have a minimum of two years of self-employment, provide two years of tax returns & Notice of Assessments and have a strong credit score.

The down payment required from the BFS borrower can be as little as 10% when they provide all the right documentation.

Trust Companies and Credit Unions require a minimum of 3 months of self-employment and often will use the cash flow coming into company bank accounts to determine applicable income.

Good credit is important and applicants with higher scores receive lower interest rates. A strong emphasis is also placed on the type, location and condition of the property being purchased.

Private Lenders (the most expensive) look for a minimum of 3 months of self-employment and alternative proof of income (billing invoices and undeclared rent are a couple of examples).

So don't despair if you are working on contract or running your own small business. BFS mortgages approved every day allowing those buyers to also enjoy the benefits of home ownership.

It makes sense however to consider that you really need to be talking to a mortgage professional about your personal situation… someone who knows and works with all the different types of lenders who will consider working with BFS applicants.

CHAPTER 17
BECOMING A TORONTO PROPERTY INVESTOR

Buying a rental property is a great way to increase wealth and invest in the real estate market.

A little planning and using a real estate professional along with a mortgage professional will help make this process a smooth and successful one.

Every market is different but the basic goal is the same… how to have your money make you money.

With a rental property, lenders consider not only the borrower's income, expenses and their credit rating but the rental potential of the property itself.

If you're looking at purchasing a multi-unit building (up to 4 units), an analysis of the income and expenses plays a major part in determining the value of that property and how much the lender will give you as a mortgage.

Other single-family properties like houses or condo suites will have their value determined strictly by what other similar homes have sold for in the very recent past.

Another big consideration is deciding on what type of return are you looking for and the length of time you want to hold onto that investment.

Returns will vary according to the amount of down payment you put on your purchase. By the way, lenders have strict guidelines as to the minimum down payment they require when the purchase is for an investment.

Some investors want a cash-on-cash return (often very difficult in Toronto's current extremely strong seller's market. Others are not so worried about month-by-month cash flow and are more interested in long-term appreciation.

A Realtor will inform you about how much expected income could be generated by specific properties and a mortgage broker can show you how to leverage your for a down payment along with ensuring the property you buy cash flows.

Using experts on both the purchase and the mortgage financing will help make you money.

CHAPTER 18
GETTING DIVORCED?
HOW TO BUY OUT YOUR SPOUSE

Statistics don't lie and divorce statistics tell us that 50% of all marriages end in divorce.

Splitting the assets and debts is more difficult than combining the two when getting married. Lots to consider and the largest family asset, your home, is one of them.

Refinance regulations at banks do not allow for refinancing for greater than 80% of the home's value BUT done correctly one spouse can buy out the others interest in a property.

The **Spousal Buyout Program** allows one spouse to 'buy back' the family home with as little as 5% down in their portion of the home's equity. This can include payouts for debts and any amounts owing to the other spouse for their interest in the property.

The spouse keeping the home must qualify for the new replacement mortgage under bank and CMHC regulations and a legal separation agreement must be in place prior to the transfer of ownership. The separation agreement must deal with the settlement of debts, child support, alimony and how much is being paid to the other spouse for their share of the property along with other settlement items.

Both of the party's lawyers (each spouse requires a separate lawyer) will ensure their client's rights are protected.

The next steps are to have a formal purchase agreement drafted by a lawyer and an appraisal done to establish the home's value so each spouse's share of the equity can be fairly established.

Taking advantage of the services from an experienced mortgage professional will make this process much smoother during a very stressful time.

CHAPTER 19
WANT TO BUY A FIXER-UPPER BUT DON'T KNOW HOW TO PAY FOR THE RENOS?

Are you contemplating purchasing a condo or house which needs some immediate renovations?

The problem for many buyers is to find the cash to do the reno. There's a big demand on your cash reserves for the down payment, closing costs often including two land transfer taxes and then moving costs and light fix-ups.

However, there is a way to get the funds to do your required renovations without depleting all your cash or supplementing the funds you have already or without drawing down on your more expensive line of credit or credit cards.

The program is called **Purchase Plus Improvements**. The program is not meant to fix deficiencies however. The improvements need to increase the property's value after they're completed.

If you are envisioning installing a new kitchen, bathroom or flooring, you can add the improvements into the total mortgage loan amount. This program may help you to make a decision to purchase an outdated home, especially if the overall cost is in your price range.

Here's how the product works...

- The lender will need a break down of the requested improvements added into the mortgage lender's application notes, along with a copy of the renovation quotation

- The total down payment will be based as a percentage of the after-the-improvements estimated market value

- You are allowed up to 120 days after closing for the improvements to be completed

- The cost of the improvements can be up to 20% of the initial purchase price up to a maximum of $40,000

- For improvements costing under $15,000, the borrower will need to provide paid receipts or an invoice for proof of completion to get reimbursement

- For improvements costing over $15,000, the borrower will need to pay for an inspection report to show proof of completion of the renovations

- The new home owner will receive a single advance from the lender once the improvements have all been completed

Sometimes buyers don't start out looking for a home that needs some fixing but, because of affordability or a shortage of listings in the market, this becomes a best alternative for them.

If this happens to you, call your mortgage professional right away to discuss how you might structure an offer differently.

CHAPTER 20
WHAT IF YOU'RE NOT A CANADIAN CITIZEN...
CAN YOU STILL GET FINANCING?

There are definitely ways for non-citizens to arrange financing for real estate purchases in Canada. These rules are divided according to the immigration status of the mortgage applicant.

New To Canada - Permanent Residents

Client Profile

Applicant must be in Canada less than 5 years

Must have established residence in Canada and obtained Permanent Residence Status

Minimum 3 months of full time employment

Down Payment

All monies must be in a Canadian bank account for 30 days prior to closing

Insured: Minimum 5% to a maximum of $1 million purchase price

Minimum 20% for greater than $1 million

Uninsured: 35%

-Additional requirement of 12 or 24 month PIT net worth requirement (over and above the down payment)

Income

Standard – employment letter / pay stub (insured mortgages only)

Documentation Needed

Permanent Residence Form (IMM 5292/IMM 5688)

Permanent Resident Card

Passport

Credit

Canadian credit bureau will be run, bank reference letter from country of origin and/or 12 months of rent & utility payment confirmation

Non-Resident Foreign Investors

Personal Information Required

No requirement for landed status

Supporting docs – talk to your mortgage professional since these will vary on a case-by-case basis

Minimum down payment required is 35% - monies MUST be in a Canadian bank account for a minimum of 30 days prior to closing

Income verification - employment letter and pay stub required for each individual applicant

Credit – Canadian credit bureau if available - otherwise a reference letter from the buyer's home bank is required

Asset verification – confirmation of liquid assets

Miscellaneous Information and Requirements

Full appraisal required

Rentals up to 4 units

Recreational properties

Co-Ownerships – on approved list

Co-ops ineligible

NO Power of Attorney allowed – the buyer must be present in Canada for closing

Land Transfer tax as per normal (Provincial and City of Toronto as applicable)

HST on new properties due on rentals

Borrowers from the following sanctioned countries are ineligible

Iran

Syria

North Korea

Myanmar (Burma)

Sudan (including South Sudan)

Cuba (on exception)

Foreign Workers - Non-Permanent Residents Of Canada

Required

Work Permit Form (IMM 1442): must be for minimum 1 year

Applicant must have entered Canada within 5 years of application

Client must be working for minimum 3 months in Canada or be a in a corporate relocation program (exempt)

Down Payment

High Ratio Insured Mortgages: 10% (5% for very strong applicants) – maximum purchase $1 million when less than 20% down

Uninsured: 35% - maximum purchase $1.5 million

Credit

Canadian or US bureau if available and / or Reference Letter from home bank, country of origin

Income

Standard policies - employment letter / pay stub, self-employed people need to provide 2 years of their Canada Revenue Notice of Assessments

Down Payment

Must be in a Canadian bank account for a minimum of 30 days prior to closing.

CHAPTER 21
CREATE A DOWN PAYMENT EVEN IF YOU HAVE ZERO SAVED RIGHT NOW!

We Have Some Creative Ways Which Might Help!

Phil and Laura called our Hotline about an article that was in one of our recent newsletters. The article that sparked their interest was entitled "Contrary To Popular Belief... You CAN Buy A Home With Almost 'Zero' Dollars Down".

They wanted to know how this would work as the house they were renting was being sold and they were looking at the cost of moving and having to pay at least $2,200 per month to rent something else!

A brief conversation on the phone got them excited about the possibilities of buying instead of paying rent. At the Buyer Consultation which followed a few days later, one of our Buyer Specialists did a complete financial analysis for them.

Phil and Laura learned that they qualified for a large RRSP contribution and for an RRSP loan that would allow them to make that investment. With the loan and RRSP contribution in place, a large tax refund was then in the works which would provide the vast majority of their down payment. They were set to start house hunting!

Within three weeks of making that initial call, from a position of thinking that it was impossible for them to buy without having any down payment, they made an offer on the new home of their dreams.

Every year, before the end of February typically, we tell buyers that this is the perfect time of year to "create" a down payment by using their RRSP allowable contribution limit and the Federal Government's Home Buyers' Plan for first time home buyers.

First a quick review... every first-time buyer has the right to withdraw up to $25,000 from his or her RRSP at the time of a home purchase. The little-known secret is that the money does NOT need to be used strictly for the down payment on your house or condo purchase.

However, it does have to be in your RRSP for at least 90 days before pulling it out to purchase a home, so that's why you need to do some advance planning!

It also can be used to pay down other debts, pay closing costs, fund renovations, or even finance a vacation to the Bahamas (not recommended, but still possible).

CHAPTER 22
SO HOW CAN YOU CREATE A DOWN PAYMENT OUT OF 'NOTHING'?

The first step is to dig out your last Tax Assessment form from CRA (you received this when you got your tax refund last spring) and check it to find out your allowable RRSP contribution as of right now.

Many people have several thousand dollars left that they can contribute because they haven't topped up their contributions annually; some people have a lot more than that.

Let's assume for a moment that a couple is planning to purchase a home and each of them can top up their RRSP by at least $25,000.

The next step is to arrange for an RRSP loan of $25,000 each. Pretty well everyone can qualify for this loan because the banks keep your RRSP investment (a GIC, for instance) in their bank, so it's safe in their eyes.

You have a couple of choices. Take out this loan for a long term (three to 10 years), not because you're going to have this loan for a long time, but because it will make your payments lower while you do have the loan. Or… take it out with a short 6 – 12 month amortization and use it as an enforced savings program.

Pay down that loan as much as possible so that when you do withdraw the money from your RRSP you'll have built up a good chunk of savings there!

When March 1st comes along, file your tax return right away and wait for the fat refund cheque to come in the mail or direct deposit into your bank account.

Let's assume that you're in a 40 per cent tax bracket. You should then get back approximately $10,000 each in tax refund based on reducing your taxable income by $25,000. This $10,000 each (total of $20,000) now becomes your down payment... don't spend it!

Now here comes the fun part. Go out and purchase a home with a closing date of at least 90 days after you put your borrowed funds into your RRSP.

When you get to about 10 days to 2-weeks prior to the closing date for your home deal, instruct the bank to cash in your $25,000 worth of RRSPs each. The person at the bank, of course, will say... "You've got a loan against it" and then you will say "Pay the loan off with the $25,000 I'm withdrawing."

Following all of these steps carefully will leave you in the enviable position of having NO RRSP loan, $20K in your hand to use as your down payment (plus any equity you've built up by paying down the loan balance) and 15 years to repay the $50,000 that you withdrew from your RRSPs (about $3,333 per year).

We've created a free downloadable report that explains this entire process. Go to **FreeGovernmentMoneyReport.com** to get your copy today.

CHAPTER 23
CASH BACK ON CLOSING…

What if you're short of cash for your closing costs?

In addition, you could combine this down payment "creation" plan with a 'cash back' plan from a financial institution to help cover your closing costs. As an example, if you take out a mortgage with some financial institutions at the posted five-year rate, you may be able to get a small percentage of the mortgage principal amount as cash back in your hand on the day of closing.

This is just one example of how our three-plus decades in real estate and our past mortgage experience can benefit you when you buy your home.

We'll bet some of our own money that no bank will tell you about this "creating" a down payment plan!

If you'd like to benefit even more from our years of experience, you might want to come in for a personal, one-on-one Buyer Consultation or Mortgage Consultation.

CHAPTER 24
PROTECT YOURSELF FROM MORTGAGE RATE INCREASES FOR A FULL 3 MONTHS!

Avoid Paying More Interest In A Rising Market... Lock In Today's Low 5-Year Mortgage Rate Regardless Of What Happens In The Next 90 Days!

If you wait to fix or lock in a mortgage rate until just before you buy, you may end up spending thousands more in interest over the life of your mortgage.

Most people are not used to thinking four months ahead but, if you are considering purchasing a home in the next 90 days, it might be the prudent thing to guarantee yourself the lowest possible rate.

Historically lenders have often only been willing to lock in, or guarantee, the 5-year mortgage rate for 60 days. The problem with that is, for buyers purchasing a little farther out, a mortgage rate could not be set. The risk was that rates would rise, causing either the home of their dreams to become more expensive on a monthly basis OR even become out of reach because of mortgage qualification guidelines.

Now, Toronto's Real Estate Team and George Christopoulos have negotiated an agreement with several of the 'big five' banks to allow our clients to lock in the rate for a full three months. With rate hikes uncertain at any time, the prudent thing for any buyer to do would be to protect themselves and get a 90-Day Rate Lock Guarantee.

In addition, if you do purchase say, 7 months from the date you get your rate lock set up, George, our Mortgage Centre lender representative, may be able to go back 90 days and give you the best rate that was available in that period. This is a big deal!

In a rising rate market, almost every lender will NOT backdate if you purchase outside of their initial 60 or 90 day rate lock period. They will only give you the then current rate.

Best of all... there's no cost and no obligation to purchase a home in that time. It is just a terrific protection in case you do!

To get started, all you have to do is let us know you'd like a free 90 Day Rate Lock Guarantee by filling in the form below.

Our mortgage professional will call you back to talk about your needs and preferences in a mortgage and then he'll lock in the rate for you.

This 90-Day Rate Lock Guarantee could save you thousands of dollars in interest over the five-year term of your mortgage! Don't settle for what the typical bank offers when you can have access to the best mortgage rate lock available in Toronto for FREE!

Here's How It Works

To get started, all you should do is let us know you'd like a free 90-Day Rate Lock Guarantee by filling in the form below.

Our mortgage lender will call you back to talk about your needs and preferences in a mortgage and then he'll lock in the rate for you.

This **90-Day Rate Lock Guarantee** could save you thousands of dollars in interest over the five-year term of your mortgage!

Don't settle for what the typical bank offers when you can have access to the best mortgage rate lock available in Toronto for FREE!

Yes, I'd like a FREE 90 Day Rate Lock Guarantee!

Name	
Address	
City	
Postal Code	
Daytime Phone	
Email	
Occupation	
Years There	
Gross Annual Income	$
Other Family Income	$
TOTAL Gross Annual Income	$
Down Payment Available	$

Email this information to **George@YourMortgageWatch.ca** to guarantee your rate!

CHAPTER 25
HOW TO 'CHEAT' ON YOUR MORTGAGE

Typically when a person talks to their banker about mortgages, most often the discussion revolves around having a standard monthly payment with an amortization of 25 years. For a $500,000 mortgage at a 3.19% interest rate, that would mean your mortgage would be paid off in full by the end of the 25th year!

However it also means that you would have paid the bank back $725,000 over that 25 year period - $500,000 in principal loan repayment AND $225,000 in interest payments!

There are several, almost secret, options available which will reduce the total interest you pay and in one case substantially reduce the interest paid by over $55,000 in the above example.

First off, let me say this. Almost every bank has these options but they aren't usually talked about unless you ask questions. The sooner you can start increasing your principal repayments, both in size and frequency, the more interest you'll save.

This is because any mortgage payment is comprised mostly of interest during the first five to ten years. However, any extra payments you make, over and above the regular payment, go directly to a reduction of the principal balance owing.

The first option that you can use is to change your payment method from monthly to accelerated bi-weekly. That means you take your monthly payment, divide it in half, and pay that amount EVERY 14 DAYS. By doing this you will make 26 payments per year and reduce the amortization significantly down to 21.8 years and save you about $30,000 of interest.

Don't take the regular bi-weekly option where you pay on the 1st and the 15th day of the month... 24 payments during the year. This method DOES NOT shorten your amortization so we don't recommend it at all.

Another option is to pay weekly ... divide your monthly payment by 4 and pay that amount every 7 days ... thereby making 52 payments during the year. This does shorten the amortization down to 21.5 years. Since this is not a significant improvement from the accelerated bi-weekly option, we suggest just to stick with the 'every 14 day' payment schedule.

Many banks will also allow you to 'double up' your bi-weekly payment and also make lump sum payments annually totaling up to 10, 15 or 20% or more of the original principal amount. You can take advantage of any of these pre-payment privileges without any penalty whatsoever.

You can also start off your mortgage with a shorter amortization. That means you will pay a higher monthly or bi-weekly payment but you WILL pay off your mortgage sooner and save lots of interest. The only disadvantage with this is that if something happens to your income... you lose a job or get injured... you cannot then make the amortization longer to reduce your payments. You're locked in.

We suggest that you set your mortgage up at the beginning for a 25-year amortization. Then take advantage of all the pre-payment privileges that you can!

The most dramatic way to save interest on your mortgage, and cheat the bank out of literally tens of thousands of dollars in interest, is to use our trademarked 'Mortgage Terminator Program'.

This Program shows you how to pay your mortgage off in just 10 years... without you winning the lottery! There are two simple steps... First make sure you're making your payments accelerated bi-weekly which reduces your amortization to 21.8 years. The second step is to increase your accelerated bi-weekly payment by 10% each and every year.

OR... not as good, but better than doing nothing - pay a lump sum every year on the 'anniversary' of the mortgage starting. If you paid $3,000 per year, your amortization would be shortened to 19 years and you'd save

$55,000 of interest. If you paid $5,000 per year, you'd be down to 18 years and a saving of almost $66,000 in interest (total interest paid over the 18 years = $159,000).

The best part of any of these options... they're all legal and no special permission is required to invoke any of them! Don't pay the banks any more interest than you have to.

CHAPTER 26
CHOOSING A MORTGAGE BROKER OR BANKER TO WORK WITH – HINT… IT'S NOT JUST ABOUT THE RATE!!

The role of a mortgage broker is to provide their client with the best possible mortgage for which they qualify. That doesn't always translate into the lowest rate.

But GDS, TDS, LTV and all of the other industry acronyms aside, what is the best mortgage for the borrower and what does the broker need to do to arrange it for them?

The first question a client (or real estate agent) will ask a broker is, "What is your rate?" Any broker who provides a number without asking some questions first is doing a disservice to their potential clients. But the rate is the rate is the rate. Or is it?

Financial institutions advertise a posted rate. Who pays the posted rate? Anyone who doesn't ask if the institution can do better (more on this later). There are a number of websites that advertise mortgage rates well below "posted rates".

Many of these discounted rates are available to most mortgage brokers (and the public). Some rates are even lower. How do you get those rates? In many instances, the broker is buying down the rate with his commission. A good deal for the client? Maybe.

If you are shopping on rate alone, you may discover surprises later on. It's like buying a car. The car is advertised at $10,000. Are you planning to drive it? You will need an engine and some wheels. Suddenly, that car costs $20,000.

Let's say a particular mortgage is advertised at 3.19 per cent. Do you plan on moving in the next five years? If so, this may not be the right product for you. The penalties to break a contract mid-term could be excessive.

In Ontario, the Financial Services Commission requires that mortgage brokers take steps to ensure the mortgage arranged is "suitable" for their client. (Similar legislation is in place across Canada.) What is the difference between "qualified" and "suitable"? The lender says, "You can have it." The borrower says, "I'll take it." So who are we to tell them it is not suitable?

Knowing the differences between lender products, as well as having a sound understanding of the clients' circumstances, could prevent a lot a grief and expense in the future. It's not just the penalties for breaking a contract that we need to be concerned with.

There are certain qualifying ratios that the industry uses when approving mortgages. Just because someone qualifies for a mortgage, doesn't mean they are comfortable carrying that much of a debt load. What if their circumstances were to change? (Loss of job, loss of income due to maternity leave, higher interest rates.)

Just like a doctor asks what the patient's 'symptoms' are before offering a diagnosis, a prudent mortgage broker will initiate these discussions before asking their clients to commit to taking on a large amount of debt.

Posted rates play a huge part in calculating pre-payment penalties. Most people are under the impression a mortgage is open on a three-month interest penalty. A mortgage is a contract. You agree to pay interest at a set rate, for a set term. If the mortgage does not specifically address early payout, you could be required to pay interest until maturity.

Most mortgages require a payment of the GREATER of three month's interest or the interest rate differential (IRD) for the remainder of the term. How does one calculate the IRD? There are no rules. The lender can use any calculation they choose. This is where the posted rate MAY affect your discharge fee.

If they have a discounted mortgage, the lender may look to re-coup the discount as part of their calculation. It is not as simple as difference in rates over the remaining term. A prudent mortgage broker will explain these nuances as part of the interview process.

The mortgage industry is changing. Technology is changing the way business is done. Bank lenders are often tripping over themselves to give discounts in the hopes of attracting new clients (only to reward loyalty by offering the posted rate on renewal to those same clients who religiously made payments for the past 60 months).

Brokers are discounting the rates even more, using rate-comparison websites. Information for consumers is everywhere (and it must be true, because it is on the Internet). Lenders are promising commitments within four hours of applying (though not necessarily consecutive hours). And in all this rush to save money quickly, the world around us is becoming more complex.

As a borrower, you are about to make one of the biggest financial decisions of your life. What's the rush? Slow down. Get all the information you need from a trained professional. They have a fiduciary responsibility to help you make the right decision. Don't be blinded by the rate. A mortgage is more than a number.

Worst Thing About Getting A Mortgage?

Over 75% of borrowers are overwhelmed by the amount of mortgage information that they need to sift through, including anything they find online and the amount of paperwork and documentation required.

There are new words and phrases to learn and understand and find out how to compare what often seems like 'apples and oranges' borrowing situations.

Make sure you understand your personal finances… create that budget we talked about earlier.

Think about how long you anticipate living in the condo or house. That may affect your making a decision about taking a variable-rate versus a fixed interest rate mortgage.

Remember, NO questions are too small or silly. Ask your mortgage broker or banker any and all questions you have. A service oriented one will take the time to give you the answers you need to have complete clarity.

Getting A Second Opinion

If you've been quoted a rate and offered a mortgage 'Quick Qualifier' certificate from a bank representative, it's quite often a good idea to get a second opinion from a professional mortgage broker as to what your interest rate and mortgage options might be.

You're certainly free to get a mortgage from whomever you want but, because getting that second opinion is free and doesn't cost you anything, doesn't it make sense to learn what that mortgage professional has to say about your situation?

You might be pleasantly surprised.

CHAPTER 27
HOW T0 PAY YOUR MORTGAGE OFF IN JUST 12-15 YEARS

We have developed a new program called the Mortgage Terminator Program. This program is designed to help any homeowner pay off their mortgage principal entirely in 10 years or less. Best of all... you can do this without making ANY lump sum payments whatsoever!

Check out the numbers shown on page 44-46 to get a feel for the impact of doing this with your mortgage.

The major benefits of the Mortgage Terminator Program are...

1. It reduces your total interest cost, saving you potentially tens (and even into the hundreds) of thousands of dollars.

2. It builds equity in your home faster (vs. paying more of your payment money towards interest).

3. You will become debt free sooner - because you're paying off your mortgage so much quicker.

4. Our Mortgage Terminator customized spreadsheet will provide you with a complete accounting - record keeping system which will track your progress, verify your mortgage lender is calculating your principal reduction accurately and provide you with the necessary documentation to detect and resolve lender errors should they occur.

5. It eliminates the cost of financing your almost forgotten CMHC mortgage insurance premium sooner.

6. You have complete control over determining how many extra principal payments you wish to make, and when.

Build Equity For Retirement OR To Move Up To That New Home In Three - Five Years!

Consumers of the "new millennia" are taking a different look at their financial realities. The dramatic changes within the economy and real estate markets have significantly changed our outlook for long-term financial security. For many, the accumulation of debt and refinancing (in some cases combined with the loss of home value) have tampered with our financial assets, not to mention our confidence and mental state.

This need not be the case. Basic mortgage planning and proper record keeping will pay off.

Prepaying the mortgage principal is an old idea that, if applied correctly, can take on new value literally! However, most consumers think of potentially making those principal payments in the form of a 'lump sum'.

But there's the problem... they just 'think' about it! Bank statistics show that 90+% of mortgage borrowers DO NOT take advantage of any lump sum payment privileges in their mortgage!

If you have a strong desire to take control of your financial future, become debt free, build your net worth and establish your financial independence, the Mortgage Terminator Program is a systematic, objective oriented tool that will enable you to achieve those goals.

Are You An Existing Homeowner With A Mortgage?

Would you like to receive by mail a free copy of the Mortgage Terminator brochure and the fill-in Information Summary Sheet?

Please go to **MortgageTerminator.LivingInToronto.com** to fill in the form to send to us. Once you fill in the Information Summary Sheet and submit it to us, we'll prepare, at no cost or obligation, a custom Mortgage Terminator spreadsheet specifically designed for your home's current mortgage.

It will show exactly what your bi-weekly mortgage payments should be adjusted to AND what your projected mortgage interest savings could be if you implemented the Mortgage Terminator Program!

CHAPTER 28
IS 'YOUR' AGENT REALLY WORKING FOR YOU?

You wouldn't -- for a lot of good reasons -- go into a contested divorce proceeding without an attorney, or worse, take the advice of your spouse's attorney.

Why, then, would you buy a home -- an adversarial process regardless of how friendly everyone involved in the transaction seems -- without someone on your side?

Oh, you think home buyers have always had representation? Well, think again.

As a buyer, you are not represented unless you've told the real estate agent who is showing you homes that you want that agent to represent you as your "buyer agent." If you haven't, "your agent" could be representing the seller.

Recently, more home buyers have been asking, "Who represents whom?" As a result, many are opting to be represented by a buyer's agent to take them through the process, from house hunting to closing.

The greatest thing about buyer representation is it doesn't cost the purchaser anything and often saves them thousands from the purchase price.

The Way We Were

Until 1995 in Toronto, real estate was sold the way it always had been -- the listing agent obtained the listing from the seller and represented that seller. A second agent, the "selling agent," brought the buyer to the table, but was acting as a sub-agent (an agent of the listing agent) often unbeknownst to the buyer.

In this situation, even though the selling agent may have never met the seller, he or she still had a legal obligation to report to the seller any information the buyer revealed, or any information the agent found out about the buyer's situation that would help the seller's negotiating position.

That makes the agents sound evil, but in fact, if they had not communicated the information to the seller, they would have been breaking the law.

Both agents had a fiduciary obligation -- a legal and moral obligation to work toward the best interests of the beneficiary. The seller was the client for whom agents were working. The buyer was merely the customer.

The Revolution Begins

In 1983, however, a classic study started a revolution in real estate sales. The Federal Trade Commission in the USA found that 72 percent of all buyers believed the agent they worked with was representing their interests.

That meant that three out of four buyers were "spilling their guts to agents who weren't representing them," as one buyer agent wrote. The report fueled a nationwide legislative agenda that forced the real estate industry to disclose whom the broker or licensee represents in every situation. By 1988, most US states had disclosure laws in place.

The executive director of the 60,000 + member Real Estate Buyer Agent Council (REBAC), says times have changed.

A survey conducted in 2003 found almost 60 percent of home buyers used buyer representation and that number is over 95% today.

REBAC trains Realtors how to serve the buyer and grants the respected Accredited Buyer Representative (ABR) designation to agents for reaching certain education and experience standards.

Buyer representation is not the exception anymore, it's the norm. Consumers now know they have the right to be represented.

Telling It Like It Is

In some provinces you can still work under the old sub-agent system, or you can choose to have buyer representation. Many provinces (including the Province of Ontario) and the Canadian Real Estate Association Realtor Code of Ethics, however, now require "Disclosure of agency" by which any agent is required to disclose his or her legal relationship with a buyer or seller "at first substantive contact".

If you, as a prospective buyer or seller, start telling an agent information that would compromise your bargaining position in any way, the agent should immediately explain "agency" and give you a choice in how you want to move forward. Unfortunately, some agents don't, so it's up to you to protect yourself.

Any licensed real estate agent in Ontario can legally act as a "buyer's agent," although not all have experience doing so.

You will be asked to sign a Buyer Representation Agreement (BRA) which states that the agent is representing YOUR interests in the complete transaction—finding out the back-story on the property, researching the actual market value of the home and negotiating the transaction—ALL on YOUR behalf!

Members of Toronto's Real Estate Team are certified buyer agents and have taken the courses necessary to obtain their **ABR** (Accredited Buyer Representative) designation. Buyer agent team members act as exclusive buyer agents for our house or condo purchasers.

Why Choose A Buyer's Agent?

While any agent will arrange property showings, suggest sources of financing, provide accurate information, explain the forms and agreements, and monitor the entire process, a buyer's agent should perform services for you that many the seller's agents can't, such as show you reasons not to buy a particular property and negotiate the best price and terms for you.

A good buyer agent will include conditions in the contract that protect you, rather than the seller as in most standard contracts; and keep confidential any information that could hurt your bargaining position.

Other Types Of Agency Representation

What if the house you want is listed by the same agent or firm that's representing you as buyer's agent? In that case, you can agree to:

Disclosed Dual Agency, in which the agent represents both you and the seller. This is absolutely NOT recommended because the listing agent's first loyalty, by agency law, is to the seller, not to you as the buyer.

Designated Agency, in which your agent continues to represent you while another agent in the same firm represents the seller. This is not uncommon and, if you're happy with the integrity of your buyer agent, you can rely on them to NOT pass any confidential information about you over to the seller's agent.

You Get What You Pay For

One thing hasn't changed: In most cases, the seller is going to pay an average of 5 percent of the sales price to a real estate firm. Almost all sellers agree to allow the listing agent to split the commission with the buyer's agent, which means the seller is paying the buyer's agent to represent the buyer against the seller.

While many people think that whoever is paying the lawyer or agent is the one getting the best representation, courts have made clear that paying an agent does not automatically mean the payor is the client.

Why would a seller agree to allow half of the commission to go to a buyer's agent who is representing a buyer against the seller? Simple -- the seller wants to sell. And as some real estate agents note, the transaction really funds the commission.

The whole idea here is fairness: If the buyer is bringing the money to the table to buy the house, shouldn't that buyer get representation? Finally, after nearly a century, the answer is yes.

The struggle is over. Buyer agency is here to stay. We still need to educate the consumer but buyer agency has come of age!

CHAPTER 29
CHOOSING THE RIGHT PROFESSIONAL AGENT IS NOT EASY

The Toronto Real Estate Board now has well over 50,000 licensed Realtors registered to work in the GTA area, up from just 28,000 less than 6 years ago.

Of those, 80+% sell less than 5 homes per year and almost 50% don't even sell 2 homes annually. Many of those agents are working at a full-time job for their income and try to do their real estate business on the side, part-time.

There are however a solid core of professional, full-time Realtors who do most the sales in the Toronto MLS. And there's an even smaller group of agents who work with a 'By Referral Only' philosophy and mind-set.

Realtors who work with this philosophy guiding their business have a keen desire to satisfy their client's every need because a clear majority of their business comes from repeat business and referrals from their happy clients. Everything they do in their real estate business is intended to provide excellent advice and counsel and add value to their client relationships.

They also know that, even if you decide not to make a move in real estate right away, that's fine. Those 'By Referral Only' agents are in the business for the long term and they'll be ready when you are – keep this criteria in mind when making the decision for which Realtor is best to represent you.

Of course, we'd love to work with every single one of you in your condo or house search, but sometimes that's not possible. You might be planning to purchase in Hamilton or Oshawa or another geographic area that we don't service.

So, take advantage of the information I'm sharing with you here and use it as a benchmark or a guideline when you are looking for a buyer agent to represent you.

Of course, when buying your Toronto condominium or house, you always have four choices…

- You could decide to do nothing… after hearing what the market is doing or finding out how much you might qualify for with a mortgage right now, you may make the decision to hold off on purchasing

- You could try to buy a home by yourself… every year about 5% of Toronto sales are made by people purchasing on their own

- You may decide to work with one of the 50,000+ agents now registered with the Toronto Real Estate Board, many of whom have very little if any experience in all the facets of property ownership and effectively helping buyers obtain their dream home

- OR you may decide to work with a **'By Referral Only' Realtor** like myself… someone whose goal is to provide such exceptional buying advice and service that you'll feel compelled to refer all your friends and family for years to come.

TO SUMMARIZE...

Has this 'Home Buyer's Financing Guide' book been of value to you? We're sure that your answer is "yes!"

What this book really illustrates is the level of service that Toronto's Real Estate Team is willing to offer to ensure that you have the best possible information available to you when we are your Realtors.

Our goal is to help you learn and be able to articulate what your goals and dreams are as they relate to real estate and your family!

When you are thinking about selling your home, picture yourself six months to a year from now. What do you see? What vision do you have of where you want to live? What does your future look like?

Maybe you need more information from us before you can do that projection into the future, such as learning if it's possible for you to purchase a home.

We are here to be your real estate information resource centre -- not to rush you into making a rash or quick decision.

You'll find that we'll not pressure you in any way, but don't misinterpret this lack of pressure for lack of interest on our part.

The interest is certainly there and our level of personal involvement will increase when you ask for it... as you come closer to the time for getting serious about buying a condominium or house!

You will get periodic phone calls from us inquiring "How is it going?" or "How can we help you?" but we are patient.

We're in the real estate business for the long term. You know we will always give you super service because we want you to become a 'Client For Life'... not just a client for one transaction.

Once you experience that difference, you won't ever want to talk to another Realtor. There just isn't a need!

We're excited about working with you and helping you out. That's where the fun is for us in this business!

All the best,

Thomas Cook and the members of Toronto's Real Estate Team

HERE'S THE FREE STUFF YOU CAN GET FROM US

Helping Toronto Home Buyers & Sellers Achieve Their Goals Since 1980

As a successful Toronto Realtor helping condo and house buyers and sellers since 1980, I've developed many programs and services to assist people with their real estate needs. Here are some of the plans of action I have designed to help.

Exclusively For Toronto Condo Or House SELLERS...

Sometimes people start thinking about selling their property years ahead of time and others jump right in and sell their condo or house within a few days or weeks.

Do you like to understand how something works before committing to it?

Either way, it makes sense to spend some time learning the right way to sell and avoiding making costly mistakes on one of the biggest sales of your life.

We've written a book to completely explain the best ways to get your condo sold for a higher price. And we've got **special programs** designed to help you achieve that.

If you are going to sell your home in the next 1 to 9 months, what you undertake right now can make a difference of thousands of dollars in your sale price, and there are some simple things you can do forthwith to make sure you get "Top-Dollar" when you do sell.

Insider Tips For Getting The Best Price - The Complete Guide To Selling Your Toronto Condo

By reading this book you're on your way to helping yourself have a successful sale and getting the highest price possible. As the saying goes 'Knowledge Is Power'. In this book, I will be telling you how my Team and I approach selling Toronto homes.

I've worked through three recessions since 1980 and now one of the longest stretches of market appreciation in Toronto's history.

So, I've seen it all... extreme buyer's markets and now extreme seller's markets... but in every instance, a competent, knowledgeable Realtor adds value to every seller when they're ready to enter the market.

Download the Book for free at **GettingTheBestPrice.ca**.

Timeline = 3-6 months before selling

A Quick Way To Find Out What Your Condo or House Could Be Worth In Today's Market

Before you start making any plans to move up, move down or move out to a rental, you'll need to know a market value price for what your home is worth in today's market.

The best way to do this is to have us complete a FREE "Pin-Point Price" Analysis, where I can take a closer in-person look at your condo and prepare a very specific price for your suite. This price will be more precise than the general range that you can get automatically from any website - and we guarantee in writing to sell your condo at the "Pin-Point Price" or higher in less than 32 days.

Go online to **PinPointPriceAnalysis.com** and fill in your property's specifics... it's that easy.

Timeline = 1-12 months before selling

Increase Your Home's Value With Simple Cosmetic Fix-Ups

So, you're happy with the price you could get... what's next?

The absolute best next step is for us to do a FREE "Room-By-Room Review", where I take a 20-minute walk-thru of your condominium and make specific recommendations about which fix-ups or improvements you should (and should not) do to prepare your suite for sale. I will point out the lowest cost, highest return improvements you can make to help sell your condo quickly and for more money.

Set up your Room-By-Room Review at **RoomByRoomReview.com.**

Timeline = 1-4 months before selling

Sell Your Condo In As Little As 24 Hours - And Laugh To Yourself At How Easy It Was

Some home owners are sensitive to having a lot of people traipsing through their home or there's some limitation as to their putting the condo on the public MLS system.

If that's you, one solution is to include your condo in our "Silent Market" of condominiums that are not yet on the open market.

Because we generate so much buyer interest from our website, Facebook and Google advertising and other proactive marketing, we may be able to find a buyer for your condo without even putting it on the market... saving you both time and money.

Register your condo 'silently' for sale at **SilentMarketForCondos.com**.

Timeline = 1-3 months before deciding to put your condo on the MLS.

Exclusively For CONDO or HOUSE BUYERS...

It's often the same for buyers... sometimes they begin thinking about buying real estate years ahead and others plunge right in and purchase a new condo or house in just a few months.

It certainly is a wise idea to spend some time learning the right way to buy and avoiding making costly mistakes on one of the biggest purchases of their life.

Our **Home Buyer University** has created several ways for you to improve your knowledge about the home buying process and how Toronto's real estate market works right now.

Enroll in as many of these options as you'd like and be all set to go when the time is right for you. Under each option is a timeline of when ideally, you'd want to be taking advantage of these free services.

Perfect If You're 6-24 Months Away From Buying A Toronto Home

It always pays to get prepared. We've designed a Buyer University educational series with articles either bi-weekly or monthly designed to teach condo and house buyers about the home buying process in Toronto in a systematic way.

Go to **Home-Buyer-University.com** and complete the Buyer University registration.

Timeline = 6-24 months before purchasing

Create A Down Payment Even If You Have Nothing Saved Right Now

Would you like to buy your first Toronto condo or house but don't have a large, or any, down payment saved right now?

Our **Free Government Money Report** will show you how to grow or add to your down payment if you're a first-time home buyer.

Download it for free at **FreeGovernmentMoneyReport.com**.

Timeline = 6-24 months before purchasing

Home Buying Advice For 1st-Time Or Experienced Buyers

Do you like to understand how something works before committing to it?

The **Ultimate Toronto Home Buyer's Guide** will take you through the entire home buying process in a comprehensive way and help take away the stress of buying one of the most expensive purchases in your lifetime.

Download the Guide for free at **UltimateHomeBuyersGuide.com**.

Timeline = 3-18 months before purchasing

Get MLS Listings Sent To You Daily Just Like Realtors See

The customized **HOMEWatch Program** is perfect if you are several months away from seriously starting your home search.

Instead of randomly looking for homes on your own, you'll get information by email on all the new listings that come on the market in any price range and Toronto neighbourhood you choose.

Go to **CustomHomewatchSearch.com**.

Timeline = 3-12 months before purchasing

Beware Of Making Significant Home Buying Errors

Buying a home can be a confusing enterprise and many people don't know the best place to start. A **Starbucks Strategy Session** is a casual over-a-coffee conversation where you'll get your big and small questions answered to give you some terrific clarity about what to do next.

Remember, to achieve any goal you need a plan. The Starbucks Strategy Session is the best first step in setting up that plan.

Sign up at **StarbucksStrategySession.com**.

Timeline = 4-16 months before purchasing

Become A Competent Authority On Determining Value

When most folks are just starting to think about buying a condo or house, they typically don't have an accurate idea of what they can get for the money. They're often worried that they're too far away from the time they want to seriously start looking and don't want to bother an agent to see some homes just for the experience.

The Market Experience Tour is designed to help you get a feel for what's out there in the market in the neighbourhoods and price ranges that you feel comfortable with, without you having to worry about bringing your cheque book along.

This Tour is not designed to find your dream home... it provides an opportunity for you to get educated and find out what home styles, layouts and price ranges work best for you well before you're ready to seriously start your home search.

Market Experience Tours happen almost every day of the week… just pick the time, price range and neighbourhoods that suit your lifestyle.

When's the best time for you to check out some neighbourhoods? Choose at **MarketExperienceTour.com**.

Timeline = 4-16 months before purchasing

How Large A Mortgage Do You Qualify For?

Often people mistakenly think that going to an online site or having a quick, casual conversation with a bank rep to find out everything they need about getting a mortgage approval but this is absolutely not the case.

The perfect solution to getting a full mortgage pre-approval is to have a private, in-depth conversation with a mortgage professional who will review your personal financial situation and offer options about the best way to move forward.

A typical Mortgage Consultation takes about 20-30 minutes and you'll walk away with a mortgage pre-approval that you can feel confident about..

Set up that very important step at **FullMortgagePreApproval.com**.

Timeline = 3-9 months before purchasing

Get Your Free 'Guide To Downtown Toronto Condo Prices'

Almost every buyer of a downtown condominium suite starts off with questions about which neighbourhood will fit their lifestyle and budget the best.

Up till now, there's been no comprehensive real estate market summary of the several downtown Toronto Real Estate Board sub-districts east and west of Yonge Street.

This expert guide is focused on giving you the data you need to make a smart condo buying decision and it's easy (and free) to download.

To become confident about where to make your downtown condominium purchase, you can get your copy of the 'Guide To Downtown Toronto Condo Prices' here...

GuideToDowntownTorontoCondoPrices.com

Timeline = 4-6 months prior to purchasing

Here's A Simple Way To Save Time And Money When Starting Your Home Search

OK, so now you're ready to start seriously looking for your new home.

You've read up about how the home buying process works, you've been receiving some targeted listings from various Toronto neighbourhoods, you've been on a few (or several) Market Experience Tours to get a feel for the current market and your full mortgage pre-approval is in place.

The next big step is to meet up with your buyer agent for a comprehensive, in-office or online Buyer Consultation so you're fully prepared when you hit the bricks looking for that perfect condo or house.

A **Buyer Consultation** with an experienced, professional agent should take approximately 60 minutes... there's a lot to cover and understand and you don't want to make any mistakes or get stressed out in the process.

Go to **BuyerConsultation.com.**

Timeline = 3-5 months before purchasing.

YOU ABSOLUTELY, POSITIVELY NEED TO KNOW WHAT THESE MEAN

As you're considering selling your home in today's busy market, even though you're already a home owner, you might want to re-familiarize yourself with the terms of the business so that you will be speaking the same "language" as the mortgage financing professionals in the field!

Mortgage Terms You Should Know

Mortgagee:
The lender (bank or trust company generally).

Mortgagor:
That's you, the borrower.

Blended Payments:
Equal payments monthly or bi-weekly consisting of both a principal and an interest component, paid each month or every two weeks during the term of the mortgage.

Because the principal is being paid down incrementally with each payment, the principal portion of that fixed payment increases each month, while the interest portion decreases, but the total monthly payment does not change.

Closed Mortgage:
A mortgage that cannot be prepaid, renegotiated or refinanced.

Most bank and institutional mortgages we see today are closed with partial pre-payment privileges built into them. If after a few years, you won the lottery and wanted to pay your mortgage off in full, the bank would charge you a penalty.

Open Mortgage:
A mortgage that can be prepaid at any time, without penalty. These are usually private mortgages which have an 'open' privilege.

Mortgage Term:
In a mortgage, "term" is the actual length of time for which the money is loaned, at that rate of interest. At the end of the term, you can either repay the balance of the principal then owing in full or, most commonly, renegotiate the mortgage at the then-current interest rates.

A typical term is 5 years, with anything from 6 months to 5 years also being available.

Amortization:
The number of fixed payments or years it takes to repay the entire amount of the mortgage loan. In Canada, this it typically 25 years.

Principal Balance:
The amount you still owe the lender at any specific time.

Interest Rate:
The return the lender receives for loaning you the money for the mortgage.

Interest rates were as high as 18-21% back in the early 1980's and were in the 4-5% range in the early 2000's. Rates over the past few years have been at record low levels in the mid- to high-2%'s.

Amortization Schedule:
The amortization schedule separates out the monthly installment portions for both principal and interest and how much of the payment is allocated to each. It also shows the unpaid principal balance.

The amortization is the number of years that it will take to pay off the mortgage, were the interest rate to remain constant. Mortgage term refers to the length of time a particular interest rate will be in effect.

Conventional mortgage:
A mortgage loan that does not exceed 80% of the appraised value or purchase price of the property, whichever is the lesser. Mortgages that exceed this must be insured and are called high-ratio mortgages.

High-Ratio Mortgage:
This is a mortgage that is higher than 80% of the purchase price (or appraised value) of the property. A high-ratio mortgage typically can be as high as 95% of the value (and in some cases, can go to 100% of value). High-ratio mortgages MUST be insured by either CMHC or one of the other two high-ratio mortgage insurers we have available in Ontario.

Mortgage Insurance Premium:
A premium that is added to the mortgage and paid by the borrower over the life of the mortgage. The mortgage insurance insures and protects the mortgage lender against loss in case of default on the part of the borrower.

In our Starbucks Strategy Session or Buyer Consultation we will review what these costs could be for your situation.

Full Mortgage Pre-Approval:
Many people mistakenly believe that by just filling in an online form or having a conversation with a banker where they verbally provide data about their income and their debts is enough to go out and buy a condo or house.

It ABSOLUTELY is not enough and it's very dangerous to buy any home based on just this.

To be 100% sure of your financial capability, and get a FULL mortgage pre-approval, a prospective buyer must provide their banker or mortgage broker with proof of income, proof of down payment and have a credit bureau done. Here's what you'll need to provide…

1- A completed mortgage application form

2- For proof of income, you'll provide a copy of your employment letter, a current pay stub and your last income tax return with T4s and Notice Of Assessment from Revenue Canada

If you are self-employed, you'll need to provide a copy of three years of Revenue Canada tax assessment statements.

3- For proof of down payment, you'll provide a copy of any GICs, term deposits, or RRSPs plus a copy of your bank statement showing current cash in the bank. If you're getting funds from a family member, you'll need to provide a copy of a gift letter signed by that person.

Your lender or mortgage broker will then do a credit check and they will issue an Unconditional Pre-Approval Certificate, which is the lender's guaranteed mortgage commitment to the buyer. It is conditional only upon an appraisal or CMHC/GE Capital approval.

At our Starbucks Strategy Session or Buyer Consultation, we will elaborate on this further and help you make the next steps forward.

Gross Debt Service (GDS) Ratio:
This percentage figure is calculated by totaling the annual payments for mortgage principal, interest, realty taxes and 50% of the heating cost, divided by the gross annual income of the borrower. Most lenders prefer that the GDS be no more than 39%.

Total Debt Service (TDS) Ratio:
This percentage figure is calculated by totaling the annual payments for mortgage principal, interest, realty taxes and 50% of heating costs, PLUS annual payments for bank loans, lines of credit, credit cards & other debts, divided by the borrower's gross annual income. Lenders prefer the TDS be no more than 44%.

P and I:
Principal and interest due on a mortgage.

P I T:
Principal, interest and realty taxes due on a mortgage.

Prepayment Options:
The right to prepay specified amounts of the principal balance (typically 10 - 20% of original mortgage principal amount depending on the lender). Penalty interest rarely may be incurred on those prepayment options. You can often increase your monthly or bi-weekly payments (by from 10-100% depending on the lender) and double-up your payment anytime.

Assumption Agreement:
In this rare case, you might agree to assume an existing mortgage on the property you're buying. The assumption agreement is a legal document

signed by the home buyer that requires the buyer to assume responsibility for the obligations of a mortgage made by a former owner.

Mortgage Life Insurance:

Not to be confused with CMHC insurance, life insurance is a form of reducing term insurance recommended for the borrower. In the event of the death of the owner, or one of the owners, the insurance pays off the balance owing on the mortgage. The intent is to protect survivors from losing their homes.

Second Mortgage:

Perhaps, due to credit issues, you can only qualify for a mortgage of up to 75% of the purchase price BUT you only have a 15% down payment. You might then arrange for a second mortgage for the missing 10% of the purchase price.

A second mortgage is usually at a higher interest rate and represents the difference between the price of the house and first mortgage plus the down payment. This may be obtained from private lenders, finance companies or through lawyers and notaries.

Variable Rate Mortgage (Floating Rate):

A mortgage in which payments can be fixed from one to five years, but the interest rate could change from month to month depending on market conditions. Variable mortgage rates are determined by adding or subtracting a certain percentage from the official Bank of Canada Prime Rate.

If interest rates go down, the monthly principal is reduced; if rates go up, the monthly payments might not cover the interest owing and payments may be increased for the next term.

Seller Take Back Mortgage (or Seller Financing):

Although rare in today's low interest, busy market, the seller of a property might provide some or all the mortgage financing to get their property sold.

Default:

Non-payment of the installments due under the terms of the mortgage(s).

Discharge:

The removal of all mortgages and financial encumbrances on a property.

Discharge Penalty:
A sum of money paid to a lender for the privilege of prepaying a mortgage in part or in full.

Mortgage Broker Underwriting Fee:
A sum of money collected by some lenders to offset expenses incurred in the lending transaction.

For 'prime' mortgage borrowers, the lender pays the broker so there is no out-of-pocket cost to the borrower.

However, if the borrower has credit or other issues and the only lenders who will supply the mortgage funds are 'second' or 'third' tier lenders, then there will most likely be a fee attached to the obtaining of that mortgage commitment.

MAKE SOME NOTES HERE

www.ingramcontent.com/pod-product-compliance
Lightning Source LLC
Chambersburg PA
CBHW070101210526
45170CB00012B/696